Usage

LESSON 1

Test-taking Strategy: Understanding Verb Tenses

Verb tenses tell the time that an action takes place or that a condition is true. The verb tense used in a sentence must make sense for the idea being expressed. It must also make sense for the ideas expressed in the surrounding sentences. Read the tense categories and examples below:

♦ Simple tenses: present, past, and future.
　Present: I <u>work</u> 40 hours each week.
　Past: However, last week I <u>worked</u> 45 hours.
　Future: Next week I <u>will work</u> 52 hours.

♦ Continuing tenses: action going on for an indefinite period during the present, past, and future.
　Present Continuous: I <u>am working</u> 40 hours each week.
　Past Continuous: I <u>was working</u> 45 hours some weeks.
　Future Continuous: I <u>will be working</u> more hours.

♦ Perfect tenses: action completed during the present, past, and future.
　Present Perfect: I <u>have worked</u> 40 hours each week.
　Past Perfect: I <u>had worked</u> 35 hours last week.
　Future Perfect: I <u>will have worked</u> 40 hours this week.

Some test questions ask you to recognize which verb tenses are used correctly.

Try these sample items. Circle the <u>best answer</u> to each one. Then check your answers.

(1) Last week, my supervisor will ask me about overtime work. (2) I told her I would like more work. (3) She says to tell her how many hours I could work.

1. Sentence 1: **Last week, my supervisor will ask me about overtime work.**

　What correction should be made to this sentence?

　(1) remove the comma after <u>week</u>
　(2) change <u>supervisor</u> to <u>Supervisor</u>
　(3) change <u>will ask</u> to <u>have asked</u>
　(4) change <u>will ask</u> to <u>asked</u>
　(5) change <u>will ask</u> to <u>ask</u>

2. Sentence 3: **She says to tell her how many hours I could work.**

　What correction should be made to this sentence?

　(1) change <u>says</u> to <u>said</u>
　(2) replace <u>says</u> with <u>say</u>
　(3) change <u>says</u> to <u>was saying</u>
　(4) insert a comma after <u>her</u>
　(5) replace <u>hours</u> with <u>hour's</u>

---

1. (4) <u>Last week</u> tells you that the action occurred in the past. Therefore the simple past tense verb <u>asked</u> is needed.

2. (1) Since the conversation took place and was completed in the past, the simple past tense verb <u>said</u> is needed.

Directions: Circle the best answer to each item. Items 1 to 5 refer to the following paragraph.

(1) Today many people enjoy running in marathons. (2) However, many runners probably don't know why the races had been called "marathons." (3) These events are named for the Greek town of Marathon, where an important battle is fought in 490 B.C. (4) The Athenian army defeated the Persian army there. (5) During the battle, Athenian generals sent a runner named Phidippides 150 miles to Sparta to ask for help. (6) Later the generals sent this same messenger to Athens, 24 miles away. (7) Phidippides delivered news of the victory; then he collapses and died. (8) His bravery and endurance were honored since the first modern marathon at the 1896 Olympic Games.

1. Sentence 2: **However, many runners probably don't know why the races had been called "marathons."**

   What correction should be made to this sentence?

   (1) remove the comma after However
   (2) change the spelling of probably to probly
   (3) change don't to didn't
   (4) change had been called to are called
   (5) change had been called to will be called

2. Sentence 3: **These events are named for the Greek town of Marathon, where an important battle is fought in 490 B.C.**

   Which of the following is the best way to write the underlined portion of this sentence? If you think the original is the best way, choose option (1).

   (1) is fought
   (2) was fought
   (3) is fought,
   (4) was being fought
   (5) were fought

3. Sentence 5: **During the battle, Athenian generals sent a runner named Phidippides 150 miles to Sparta to ask for help.**

   What correction should be made to this sentence?

   (1) remove the comma after battle
   (2) change generals to Generals
   (3) replace sent with will be sending
   (4) change ask to asked
   (5) no correction is necessary

4. Sentence 7: **Phidippides delivered news of the victory; then he collapses and died.**

   Which of the following is the best way to write the underlined portion of this sentence? If you think the original is the best way, choose option (1).

   (1) delivered news of the victory; then he collapses
   (2) had delivered news of the victory; then he collapses
   (3) delivered news of the victory; then collapses
   (4) delivered news of the victory, then he collapsed
   (5) delivered news of the victory, then he would collapse

5. Sentence 8: **His bravery and endurance were honored since the first modern marathon at the 1896 Olympic Games.**

   What correction should be made to this sentence?

   (1) change were to have been
   (2) change were to will be
   (3) insert a comma after honored
   (4) replace marathon with Marathon
   (5) no correction is necessary

Items 6 to 10 refer to the following paragraph.

(1) Most people are not very familiar with the importance of automobile airbags. (2) A woman recently saw a terrifying accident in which the driver would probably have been killed if he was not protected by an airbag. (3) Instead, he will walk away with only a few bruises. (4) The woman had known that seat belts were important, and she had always buckled up. (5) Until she saw that accident, though, she hasn't thought much about airbags. (6) Now she said she will never again drive or ride in a car without airbags.

6. Sentence 2: **A woman recently saw a terrifying accident in which the driver would probably have been killed if he was not protected by an airbag.**

   Which of the following is the best way to write the underlined portion of this sentence? If you think the original is the best way, choose option (1).

   (1) killed if he was not protected
   (2) killed; if he was not protected
   (3) killed if he had not been protected
   (4) killed, if he was not protected
   (5) killed if he would not have been protected

7. Sentence 3: **Instead, he will walk away with only a few bruises.**

   What correction should be made to this sentence?

   (1) remove the comma after Instead
   (2) change the spelling of Instead to Insted
   (3) change will walk to walked
   (4) change will walk to has walked
   (5) no correction is necessary

8. Sentence 4: **The woman had known that seat belts were important, and she had always buckled up.**

   What correction should be made to this sentence?

   (1) change had known to knows
   (2) insert a comma after known
   (3) remove the comma after important
   (4) change buckled to will be buckled
   (5) no correction is necessary

9. Sentence 5: **Until she saw that accident, though, she hasn't thought much about airbags.**

   What correction should be made to this sentence?

   (1) change saw to seen
   (2) remove the comma after accident
   (3) change hasn't to hadn't
   (4) change thought to think
   (5) change thought to been thinking

10. Sentence 6: **Now she said she will never again drive or ride in a car without airbags.**

    What correction should be made to this sentence?

    (1) replace said with says
    (2) change the spelling of again to agin
    (3) change drive to have driven
    (4) change ride to been riding
    (5) no correction is necessary

Usage
L E S S O N 2

Test-taking Strategy: Understanding Irregular Verbs

All verbs have three principal parts: the present form, the past form, and the past participle form.

♦ Regular verbs add *-d* or *-ed* to the present form to make the past and past participle forms:

present	talk
past	talked
past participle	talked

♦ Irregular verbs usually change spelling to make the past and past participle forms:

present	choose
past	chose
past participle	chosen

♦ The past participle form of both regular and irregular verbs always uses a helping verb, such as *has, have, had, is, are, was,* or *were*:

have talked
were chosen

Some test questions ask you to recognize whether irregular verbs are used correctly.

Try these sample items. Circle the <u>best answer</u> to each one. Then check your answers.

(1) Have you ever made a difficult task harder by putting it off? (2) If you are like most of us, you probably done so at least once. (3) It may have took you a long time just to get started.

1. Sentence 2: **If you are like most of us, you probably done so at least once.**

What correction should be made to this sentence?

(1) change <u>are</u> to <u>is</u>
(2) remove the comma after <u>us</u>
(3) change <u>done</u> to <u>have done</u>
(4) change <u>done</u> to <u>have did</u>
(5) change the spelling of <u>least</u> to <u>leest</u>

2. Sentence 3: **It may have took you a long time just to get started.**

What correction should be made to this sentence?

(1) remove <u>have</u>
(2) replace <u>took</u> with <u>taken</u>
(3) replace <u>took</u> with <u>take</u>
(4) insert a comma after <u>you</u>
(5) insert a comma after <u>time</u>

---

1. **(3)** Since <u>done</u> is the past participle form of the irregular verb <u>do</u>, it needs the helping verb <u>have</u>. Past participle forms must have helping verbs.

2. **(2)** <u>Took</u> is the past form of the irregular verb <u>take</u>. It is not correctly used with the helping verb <u>have</u>. The past participle <u>taken</u> is the correct form.

Practice   Irregular Verbs

Directions: Circle the best answer to each item. Items 1 to 5 refer to the following paragraph.

(1) Water is important for good health. (2) By the end of each day, you should have drank six to eight glasses. (3) Water becomes especially important when you are exercising. (4) If you took in four to eight ounces of fluid before you began to exercise you still need to get that same amount every 15 minutes while you are exercising. (5) After exercising, make sure you haven't forget to drink another eight to 16 ounces of fluid. (6) You may have spent money on expensive sports drinks in the past. (7) However, you could have chose water because it is just as good as commercial sports drinks and a lot cheaper.

1. Sentence 2: **By the end of each day, you should have drank six to eight glasses.**

   Which of the following is the best way to write the underlined portion of this sentence? If you think the original is the best way, choose option (1).

   (1) day, you should have drank
   (2) day you should have drank
   (3) day; you should drunk
   (4) day, you should have drunk
   (5) day, you should have drink

2. Sentence 4: **If you took in four to eight ounces of fluid before you began to exercise you still need to get that same amount every 15 minutes while you are exercising.**

   What correction should be made to this sentence?

   (1) change took to taken
   (2) change began to begun
   (3) insert a comma after exercise
   (4) insert a comma after minutes
   (5) replace are with is

3. Sentence 5: **After exercising, make sure you haven't forget to drink another eight to 16 ounces of fluid.**

   What correction should be made to this sentence?

   (1) remove the comma after exercising
   (2) change haven't to havent
   (3) replace forget with forgotten
   (4) replace ounces with ounce
   (5) no correction is necessary

4. Sentence 6: **You may have spent money on expensive sports drinks in the past.**

   What correction should be made to this sentence?

   (1) change have spent to spend
   (2) change have spent to have spend
   (3) replace sports with sport's
   (4) change past to passed
   (5) no correction is necessary

5. Sentence 7: **However, you could have chose water because it is just as good as commercial sports drinks and a lot cheaper.**

   What correction should be made to this sentence?

   (1) remove the comma after However
   (2) replace chose with chosen
   (3) replace chose with choosed
   (4) change the spelling of because to becuse
   (5) change the spelling of a lot to alot

Tip

   Become familiar with the principal parts of common irregular verbs. Some of these irregular verbs can be grouped according to the way they change. Others do not follow a pattern.

Items 6 to 10 refer to the following paragraph.

(1) Some parents have taught their children the value of money, and the importance of saving. (2) Perhaps they know that even young children can benifit from these lessons. (3) Many experts who were writing on the subject say that parents need help teaching their children good money habits. (4) For example, preschoolers can be given piggy banks. (5) They learn to save for things they wanted such as toys, candy, and trips to a pizza restaurant. (6) Parents can then compare these things to "needs" such as basic food, clothing, and shelter. (7) When children understand the difference between wants and needs, they have began to know the basics of making a budget.

6. Sentence 1: **Some parents have taught their children the value of money, and the importance of saving.**

   What correction should be made to this sentence?

   (1) replace taught with teached
   (2) change their to there
   (3) remove the comma after money
   (4) change the comma after money to a semicolon
   (5) no correction is necessary

7. Sentence 2: **Perhaps they know that even young children can benifit from these lessons.**

   What correction should be made to this sentence?

   (1) change know to will know
   (2) change know to will have known
   (3) change the spelling of benifit to binefit
   (4) change the spelling of benifit to benefit
   (5) no correction is necessary

8. Sentence 3: **Many experts who were writing on the subject say that parents need help teaching their children good money habits.**

   Which of the following is the best way to write the underlined portion of this sentence? If you think the original is the best way, choose option (1).

   (1) experts who were writing
   (2) experts, who wrote
   (3) experts who have written
   (4) experts who will write
   (5) experts who will have written

9. Sentence 5: **They learn to save for things they wanted such as toys, candy, and trips to a pizza restaurant.**

   What correction should be made to this sentence?

   (1) change learn to learnt
   (2) insert a comma after save
   (3) change wanted to want
   (4) remove the comma after toys
   (5) change the spelling of restaurant to restarant

10. Sentence 7: **When children understand the difference between wants and needs, they have began to know the basics of making a budget.**

    Which of the following is the best way to write the underlined portion of this sentence? If you think the original is the best way, choose option (1).

    (1) wants and needs, they have began to know
    (2) wants and needs they have began to know
    (3) wants, and needs they have began to know
    (4) wants and needs, they have begin to know
    (5) wants and needs, they have begun to know

Test-taking Strategy: Understanding Sequence of Tenses

Verb tenses within a sentence and within an entire paragraph should be consistent. Do not change tenses unless the action or condition you are talking about requires it.

♦ When there is more than one verb in a sentence or paragraph, the tense of each verb tells its relationship to the other verb(s). In deciding on the proper tense, ask yourself these questions: Do the events or conditions occur at the same time or at different times? If the times are different, what is the difference?

Example: I <u>saw</u> the movie after I <u>had read</u> the book.

Explanation: Since reading the book happened before seeing the movie, but both actions happened in the past, <u>had read</u> is past perfect tense and <u>saw</u> is simple past tense.

Some test questions ask you to recognize whether tense sequence within sentences and within paragraphs is correct.

Try these sample items. Circle the <u>best answer</u> to each one. Then check your answers.

(1) Heart disease and cancer were major illnesses that affect men and women. (2) They are leading causes of death today. (3) Many scientists are working to cure these conditions.

1. Sentence 1: **Heart disease and cancer were major illnesses that affect men and women.**

   What correction should be made to this sentence?

   (1) change the spelling of <u>disease</u> to <u>disese</u>
   (2) change <u>were</u> to <u>are</u>
   (3) change <u>were</u> to <u>will be</u>
   (4) replace <u>illnesses</u> with <u>illness</u>
   (5) insert a comma after <u>illnesses</u>

2. Sentence 3: **Many scientists are working to cure these conditions.**

   What correction should be made to this sentence?

   (1) replace <u>are working</u> with <u>will work</u>
   (2) replace <u>are working</u> with <u>worked</u>
   (3) insert a comma after <u>working</u>
   (4) change <u>cure</u> to <u>will cure</u>
   (5) no correction is necessary

   ---

   1. **(2)** When you read the whole paragraph, you see that it is written in present tense. There is no reason for the verb in the first sentence to be in another tense.

   2. **(5)** The sentence is correct. The verb <u>are working</u> is present continuous tense because the action is ongoing in the present. There is no reason to add a comma or change <u>cure</u> to <u>will cure</u>.

Directions: Circle the best answer to each item. Items 1 to 5 refer to the following paragraph.

(1) An increasing amount of food is exported to the United States and Canada from the countries of south America. (2) For example, Chile grew and exports many varieties of non-tropical fruit, especially apples. (3) Table grapes and lemons are also grown for export. (4) Vineyards planted in the sixteenth century produce excellent wines. (5) In many kitchens of North America, cooks have came to rely on superb seafood from the waters off Chile's long Pacific coast. (6) The kinds and quantities of food exports will have grown beyond the coffee that we have long enjoyed from South America.

1. Sentence 1: **An increasing amount of food is exported to the United States and Canada from the countries of south America.**

   What correction should be made to this sentence?

   (1) change the spelling of amount to ammount
   (2) replace is with was
   (3) replace is with had been
   (4) insert a comma after Canada
   (5) change south to South

2. Sentence 2: **For example, Chile grew and exports many varieties of non-tropical fruit, especially apples.**

   What correction should be made to this sentence?

   (1) remove the comma after example
   (2) change grew to grows
   (3) change exports to exported
   (4) change exports to will export
   (5) change the spelling of especially to expecially

3. Sentence 4: **Vineyards planted in the sixteenth century produce excellent wines.**

   Which of the following is the best way to write the underlined portion of this sentence? If you think the original is the best way, choose option (1).

   (1) Vineyards planted in the sixteenth century produce
   (2) Vineyards, planted in the sixteenth century produce
   (3) Vineyards planted in the sixteenth century, produce
   (4) Vineyards planted in the sixteenth century will produce
   (5) Vineyards planted in the sixteenth century had produced

4. Sentence 5: **In many kitchens of North America, cooks have came to rely on superb seafood from the waters off Chile's long Pacific coast.**

   What correction should be made to this sentence?

   (1) remove the comma after America
   (2) replace cooks with cookes
   (3) change came to come
   (4) replace waters with wateres
   (5) change Pacific to pacific

5. Sentence 6: **The kinds and quantities of food exports will have grown beyond the coffee that we have long enjoyed from South America.**

   Which of the following is the best way to write the underlined portion of this sentence? If you think the original is the best way, choose option (1).

   (1) quantities of food exports will have grown
   (2) quantityes of food exports grown
   (3) quantities of food exportes will grow
   (4) quantities of food exports have grown
   (5) quantitys of food exports has grown

Items 6 to 10 refer to the following paragraph.

(1) The beaches in the southern United States along the Gulf of Mexico, are popular destinations for thousands of people each summer. (2) The sun, sand, and surf are great fun. (3) One danger that everyone must look out for when the water got very warm and salty is periodic invasions of stinging jellyfish. (4) Activities like wading, fishing, or swimming brought adults and children into contact with these creatures. (5) Jellyfish can sting dead or alive, so many stings occurred on land when people step on a jellyfish or try to pick one up. (6) Stings are painful but are usually not dangerous accept for people who have allergies.

6. Sentence 1: **The beaches in the southern United States along the Gulf of Mexico, are popular destinations for thousands of people each summer.**

   What correction should be made to this sentence?

   (1) insert a comma after beaches
   (2) change southern to Southern
   (3) remove the comma after Mexico
   (4) replace are with will be
   (5) no correction is necessary

7. Sentence 3: **One danger that everyone must look out for when the water got very warm and salty is periodic invasions of stinging jellyfish.**

   What correction should be made to this sentence?

   (1) insert a semicolon after for
   (2) change got to gets
   (3) insert a comma after warm
   (4) change is to had been
   (5) no correction is necessary

8. Sentence 4: **Activities like wading, fishing, or swimming brought adults and children into contact with these creatures.**

   What correction should be made to this sentence?

   (1) remove the comma after wading
   (2) insert a comma after swimming
   (3) change brought to bring
   (4) change children to childrens
   (5) insert a comma after contact

9. Sentence 5: **Jellyfish can sting dead or alive, so many stings occurred on land when people step on a jellyfish or try to pick one up.**

   Which of the following is the best way to write the underlined portion of this sentence? If you think the original is the best way, choose option (1).

   (1) many stings occurred on land when people step
   (2) many stinges occurred on land when people step
   (3) many sting occur on land when people step
   (4) many stings occur on land when people step
   (5) many stings occurr on land when people step

10. Sentence 6: **Stings are painful but are usually not dangerous accept for people who have allergies.**

    What correction should be made to this sentence?

    (1) change are to were
    (2) insert a comma after painful
    (3) change accept to except
    (4) replace have with had
    (5) replace allergies with allergys

Tip

Figure out when the action or condition occurs; then decide whether the verb tense matches that time.

Test-taking Strategy: Understanding Subject-Verb Agreement

♦ The subject and verb in a sentence must agree in number. This means that if the subject is singular, the verb must be singular. Likewise, if the subject is plural, the verb must be plural:

My computer is not working. (singular subject and verb)
Our computers are not working. (plural subject and verb)

♦ A compound subject joined by *and* is plural. It requires a plural verb:

The fax machine and the copier are being repaired.

♦ Singular compound subjects joined by *or* or *nor* require a singular verb:

Either the fax machine or the copier is being repaired.

♦ When a singular and a plural subject are joined by *or* or *nor*, the verb agrees with the closest subject:

Neither the fax machine nor the copiers are working.
Neither the copiers nor the fax machine is working.

Some test questions ask you to recognize whether subjects and verbs agree.

Try these sample items. Circle the best answer to each one. Then check your answers.

(1) Neither digging, planting, weeding, nor watering is optional if you are a gardener. (2) However, beautiful flowers and delicious food rewards you for all this work.

1. Sentence 1: **Neither digging, planting, weeding, nor watering is optional if you are a gardener.**

What correction should be made to this sentence?

(1) change the spelling of Neither to Niether
(2) remove the comma after digging
(3) change is to are
(4) change is to were
(5) no correction is necessary

2. Sentence 2: **However, beautiful flowers and delicious food rewards you for all this work.**

What correction should be made to this sentence?

(1) remove the comma after However
(2) change the spelling of beautiful to beutiful
(3) change the spelling of delicious to delicius
(4) replace rewards with reward
(5) insert a comma after you

1. **(5)** Since the four parts of the compound subject are joined by nor, the singular verb is is correct.

2. **(4)** The compound subject is joined by and; therefore, it is plural and requires the plural verb reward.

 **Practice** Subject-Verb Agreement

Directions: Circle the <u>best answer</u> to each item. <u>Items 1 to 5</u> refer to the following paragraph.

(1) Neither drinking nor sleeping mixes with driving. (2) Some experts view being sleepy behind the wheel like being intoxicated. (3) Driving at night or driving when you're tired increase the likelihood of an accident. (4) There have been some common danger signs that you could fall asleep while driving. (5) Yawning and noding are two signs of fatigue. (6) Drifting off the road and jerking the car back into the lane also means you are in danger.

1. Sentence 2: **Some experts view being sleepy behind the wheel like being intoxicated.**

   If you rewrote sentence 2 beginning with

   <u>For some experts, being sleepy behind the wheel</u>

   the next word should be

   (1) views
   (2) is
   (3) are
   (4) was
   (5) being

2. Sentence 3: **Driving at night or driving when you're tired increase the likelihood of an accident.**

   What correction should be made to this sentence?

   (1) insert a comma after <u>night</u>
   (2) change <u>you're</u> to <u>your</u>
   (3) change <u>increase</u> to <u>increases</u>
   (4) change the spelling of <u>likelihood</u> to <u>likelehood</u>
   (5) no correction is necessary

3. Sentence 4: **There have been some common danger signs that you could fall asleep while driving.**

   Which of the following is the best way to write the underlined portion of this sentence? If you think the original is the best way, choose option (1).

   (1) There have been some common danger signs
   (2) Their have been some common danger signs
   (3) There have been some common danger signs;
   (4) There are some common danger signs
   (5) There were some common danger signs

4. Sentence 5: **Yawning and noding are two signs of fatigue.**

   What correction should be made to this sentence?

   (1) change <u>and</u> to <u>or</u>
   (2) change the spelling of <u>noding</u> to <u>nodding</u>
   (3) replace <u>are</u> with <u>is</u>
   (4) replace <u>are</u> with <u>will be</u>
   (5) change the spelling of <u>fatigue</u> to <u>fatige</u>

5. Sentence 6: **Drifting off the road and jerking the car back into the lane also means you are in danger.**

   What correction should be made to this sentence?

   (1) change <u>road</u> to <u>rode</u>
   (2) insert a comma after <u>lane</u>
   (3) change <u>means</u> to <u>mean</u>
   (4) change <u>are</u> to <u>was</u>
   (5) no correction is necessary

   — **Tip** ——————————————
   A plural verb does not end in -s. If the subject of a sentence is plural and the verb ends in -s, you know that the subject and verb don't agree.

Lesson 4   **13**

Items 6 to 10 refer to the following paragraph.

(1) In 1755 a group of French settlers were expelled from their adopted homeland. (2) They settle earlier in what is now the Canadian province of Nova Scotia. (3) They called the coastal area where they lived Acadia. (4) However they became victims of the struggle between France and England for control of North America. (5) They scattered throughout the British colonies from Massachusetts to Louisiana. (6) The group that settled in Louisiana came to be known as "Cajuns," a word derived from "Acadians." (7) Henry Wadsworth Longfellows famous narrative poem "Evangeline" is about the French settlers transplanted to Louisiana.

6. Sentence 2: **They settle earlier in what is now the Canadian province of Nova Scotia.**

   What correction should be made to this sentence?

   (1) change settle to had settled
   (2) change is to was
   (3) change is to will be
   (4) insert a comma after province
   (5) no correction is necessary

7. Sentence 3: **They called the coastal area where they lived Acadia.**

   If you rewrote sentence 3 beginning with

   Acadia was the name they

   the next word(s) should be

   (1) had called
   (2) call
   (3) will call
   (4) give
   (5) called

8. Sentence 4: **However they became victims of the struggle between France and England for control of North America.**

   What correction should be made to this sentence?

   (1) insert a comma after However
   (2) change became to become
   (3) change became to will become
   (4) insert a comma after France
   (5) insert a semicolon after England

9. Sentence 6: **The group that settled in Louisiana came to be known as "Cajuns," a word derived from "Acadians."**

   Which of the following is the best way to write the underlined portion of this sentence? If you think the original is the best way, choose option (1).

   (1) settled in Louisiana came to be known as "Cajuns,"
   (2) will settle in Louisiana came to be known as "Cajuns,"
   (3) settled in Louisiana come to be known as "Cajuns,"
   (4) settled in Louisiana will come to be known as "Cajuns,"
   (5) settle in Louisiana came to be known as "Cajuns"

10. Sentence 7: **Henry Wadsworth Longfellows famous narrative poem "Evangeline" is about the French settlers transplanted to Louisiana.**

    What correction should be made to this sentence?

    (1) change Longfellows to Longfellow's
    (2) insert a comma after Longfellows
    (3) insert a comma after famous
    (4) change is to has been
    (5) change is to will be

Usage

Test-taking Strategy: Understanding Common
Agreement Problems

Some sentences present subject-verb agreement problems. Here are three types of problem sentences:

♦ Sentences with interrupting phrases

In these sentences, groups of words that give information about the subject separate the subject and verb:

Walking, a popular activity, is good exercise.

♦ Sentences with inverted sentence structure

In these sentences, the subject comes after the verb. Questions often have inverted sentence structure:

Near the top of the page is the date of the letter.
Has our pizza order arrived yet?

♦ Sentences that begin with expletives

The words *here* and *there* are called expletives when they begin a sentence. An expletive is not the subject of a sentence even though it comes before the verb. Look for the subject after the verb:

There will be many changes in computer technology.

Some test questions ask you to recognize whether subjects and objects agree in situations like these.

Try these sample items. Circle the best answer to each one. Then check your answers.

(1) Among the unusual experiences in Swedish Lapland are the chance to stay in a hotel built entirely of ice. (2) Have many people chosen this adventure? (3) There probably haven't been a waiting list for room reservations.

1. Sentence 1: **Among the unusual experiences in Swedish Lapland are the chance to stay in a hotel built entirely of ice.**

   What correction should be made to this sentence?

   (1) change the spelling of experiences to experences
   (2) change Swedish to swedish
   (3) insert a comma after Lapland
   (4) change are to is
   (5) no correction is necessary

2. Sentence 3: **There probably haven't been a waiting list for room reservations.**

   What correction should be made to this sentence?

   (1) replace There with Here
   (2) change the spelling of probably to probly
   (3) replace haven't with havent
   (4) change haven't to hasn't
   (5) change room to room's

   ---

   1. (4) The subject of this inverted sentence is chance, a singular noun that requires the singular verb is.

   2. (4) The subject of this sentence, which begins with the expletive there, is list, a singular noun that requires the singular verb hasn't been.

Directions: Circle the <u>best answer</u> to each item. <u>Items 1 to 5</u> refer to the following paragraph.

(1) Along with the advantages of credit cards exists potential pitfalls. (2) Charges for all kinds of things we buy adds up fast. (3) There are many of us who have enormous credit card debts. (4) The best thing we can do for ourselves is pay off the balances. (5) How much does our financial situations suffer from large credit card balances? (6) Actually, the money we pay in interest charges could be going into our pockets instead.

1. Sentence 1: **Along with the advantages of credit cards exists potential pitfalls.**

   What correction should be made to this sentence?

   (1) change the spelling of <u>advantages</u> to <u>advantadges</u>
   (2) change <u>advantages</u> to <u>advantage</u>
   (3) insert a comma after <u>cards</u>
   (4) replace <u>exists</u> with <u>exist</u>
   (5) replace <u>exists</u> with <u>existed</u>

2. Sentence 2: **Charges for all kinds of things we buy adds up fast.**

   Which of the following is the best way to write the underlined portion of this sentence? If you think the original is the best way, choose option (1).

   (1) things we buy adds up
   (2) things we buy, adds up
   (3) things we will buy adds up
   (4) things we buy added up
   (5) things we buy add up

3. Sentence 3: **There are many of us who have enormous credit card debts.**

   What correction should be made to this sentence?

   (1) change <u>are</u> to <u>is</u>
   (2) insert a comma after <u>us</u>
   (3) change <u>have</u> to <u>had</u>
   (4) change the spelling of <u>enormous</u> to <u>enormos</u>
   (5) no correction is necessary

4. Sentence 4: **The best thing we can do for ourselves is pay off the balances.**

   If you rewrote sentence 4 beginning with

   <u>Paying off the balances</u>

   the next word(s) should be

   (1) is
   (2) was
   (3) will be
   (4) are
   (5) has been

5. Sentence 5: **How much <u>does our financial situations suffer</u> from large credit card balances?**

   Which of the following is the best way to write the underlined portion of this sentence? If you think the original is the best way, choose option (1).

   (1) does our financial situations suffer
   (2) do our financial situations suffer
   (3) did our financial situations suffer
   (4) does our financial situations suffers
   (5) does our financiel situations suffer

Tip **To figure out subject-verb agreement for inverted sentences, change the sentence to normal order.**

Items 6 to 10 refer to the following paragraph.

(1) Opposite the Vietnam Memorial and near the Lincoln Memorial in Washington, D.C., is the newer Korean War Memorial. (2) It honors the 1.7 million Americans who served and the 54,000 who died in the Korean War from 1950 to 1953. (3) This conflict came soon after World War II and before the Vietnam War. (4) Overshadowed by both of these events, it has been called the forgotten war. (5) However, the Korean War Memorial, dedicated in 1995, 42 years after the war's end, now reminds everyone of that war. (6) On a long black granite wall is nineteen 7-foot soldiers trudging uphill. (7) There is an inscription at the end of the wall that reads, "Freedom is Not Free."

6. Sentence 1: **Opposite the Vietnam Memorial and near the Lincoln Memorial in Washington, D.C., is the newer Korean War Memorial.**

   What correction should be made to this sentence?

   (1) insert a comma after Vietnam Memorial
   (2) remove the comma after Washington
   (3) remove the comma after D.C.
   (4) change is to are
   (5) no correction is necessary

7. Sentence 4: **Overshadowed by both of these events, it has been called the forgotten war.**

   If you rewrote sentence 4 beginning with

   It has been called the forgotten war because

   the next words should be

   (1) it overshadowed
   (2) of these
   (3) it was
   (4) it will be
   (5) it overshadows

8. Sentence 5: **However, the Korean War Memorial, dedicated in 1995, 42 years after the war's end, now reminds everyone of that war.**

   Which of the following is the best way to write the underlined portion of this sentence? If you think the original is the best way, choose option (1).

   (1) 42 years after the war's end, now reminds
   (2) 42 years after the wars end, now reminds
   (3) 42 years after the war's end now reminds
   (4) 42 years after the war's end, now remind
   (5) 42 years after the war's end, now had reminded

9. Sentence 6: **On a long black granite wall is nineteen 7-foot soldiers trudging uphill.**

   What correction should be made to this sentence?

   (1) insert a comma after wall
   (2) change is to are
   (3) insert a comma after nineteen
   (4) change soldiers to soldiers'
   (5) no correction is necessary

10. Sentence 7: **There is an inscription at the end of the wall that reads, "Freedom is Not Free."**

    What correction should be made to this sentence?

    (1) replace the first is with are
    (2) insert a comma after wall
    (3) change reads to will read
    (4) change reads to read
    (5) no correction is necessary

Usage

LESSON 6

Test-taking Strategy: Understanding Personal Pronouns

♦ Personal pronouns can be grouped by form. Select the form depending on the way they are used in a sentence.

Subject Pronouns:	I, you, he, she, it, we, they
Object Pronouns:	me, you, him, her, it, us, them
Possessive Pronouns:	my, your, his, her, its, our, their (before nouns)
	mine, yours, his, hers, its, ours, theirs (after verbs)

♦ Personal pronouns can be grouped by person. *First person* refers to the person speaking, *second person* refers to the person spoken to, and *third person* refers to the person or thing spoken about.

First Person Pronouns:	I, me, my, mine, we, us, our, ours
Second Person Pronouns:	you, your, yours
Third Person Pronouns:	he, him, his, she, her, hers, it, its, they, them, theirs

♦ A common pronoun error is a confusing shift in person.

Example: We try to eat well because good food keeps you healthy.
Explanation: The sentence contains a confusing shift from a third person to a second person pronoun. Change you to us to correct the sentence.

Some test questions ask you to recognize whether personal pronouns are used correctly in sentences and in paragraphs.

Try these sample items. Circle the best answer to each one. Then check your answers.

(1) Both my wife and me try to exercise regularly. (2) When we don't get adequate exercise, your health suffers.

1. Sentence 1: **Both my wife and me try to exercise regularly.**

What correction should be made to this sentence?

(1) change my to mine
(2) change me to I
(3) insert a comma after me
(4) change the spelling of exercise to exerrcise
(5) no correction is necessary

2. Sentence 2: **When we don't get adequate exercise, your health suffers.**

What correction should be made to this sentence?

(1) replace don't with dont
(2) change the spelling of adequate to adequite
(3) remove the comma after exercise
(4) change your to our
(5) no correction is necessary

---

1. **(2)** The subject form of the first person pronoun is needed. I is part of the compound subject of this sentence.

2. **(4)** The pronoun our is needed to correct the confusing pronoun shift in the sentence. We and our are both first person pronouns.

Focus on Skills • Usage and Sentence Structure

Directions: Circle the best answer to each item. Items 1 to 5 refer to the following paragraphs.

(1) Experts are now advising all of us who are computer users to place their monitors below eye level and tilted away from the face. (2) Then we can read our monitors like you would read a magazine. (3) Monitors have been placed too high. (4) People have assumed that I read best at eye level, but we don't. (5) With my monitor too high, I have had neck and shoulder pain. (6) If you have had a similar experience, then you and me should listen to this new information. (7) Join me in changing our habits.

1. Sentence 1: **Experts are now advising all of us who are computer users to place their monitors below eye level and tilted away from the face.**

   Which of the following is the best way to write the underlined portion of this sentence? If you think the original is the best way, choose option (1).

   (1) of us who are computer users to place their monitors
   (2) of them who are computer users to place their monitors
   (3) of us who were computer users to place our monitors
   (4) of us who are computer user's to place their monitors
   (5) of us who are computer users to place our monitors

2. Sentence 2: **Then we can read our monitors like you would read a magazine.**

   What correction should be made to this sentence?

   (1) change we to you
   (2) insert a comma after monitors
   (3) change you to we
   (4) replace read with have read
   (5) change the spelling of magazine to magezine

3. Sentence 4: **People have assumed that I read best at eye level, but we don't.**

   What correction should be made to this sentence?

   (1) remove have
   (2) change have assumed to will assume
   (3) change I to we
   (4) change the comma to a semicolon
   (5) change don't to didn't

4. Sentence 6: **If you have had a similar experience, then you and me should listen to this new information.**

   Which of the following is the best way to write the underlined portion of this sentence? If you think the original is the best way, choose option (1).

   (1) have had a similar experience, then you and me
   (2) had a similar experience, then you and me
   (3) have had a simular experience then you and me
   (4) have had a similar experience, then you and I
   (5) have had a similar experience; then you and I

5. Sentence 7: **Join me in changing our habits.**

   What correction should be made to this sentence?

   (1) change me to him
   (2) change me to I
   (3) change our to her
   (4) change our to yours
   (5) no correction is necessary

Items 6 to 10 refer to the following paragraph.

(1) The polite behavior, or manners, expected of children has changed greatly over the years. (2) During the fifteenth century, children were expected to stand continuously in the presence of their parents, and to kneel in the presence of their teachers. (3) In the seventeenth and eighteenth centuries, a young man could not speak to a young woman until they had been properly introduced. (4) Then the first move was hers since he could not speak to her until she had acknowledged his first. (5) Today the rules are much less rigid, but them do exist in some fashion. (6) Recognizing and following it is important for acceptable social behavior.

6. Sentence 2: **During the fifteenth century, children were expected to stand continuously in the presence of their parents, and to kneel in the presence of their teachers.**

   What correction should be made to this sentence?

   (1) remove the comma after <u>fifteenth century</u>
   (2) change <u>presence</u> to <u>presents</u>
   (3) change <u>their parents</u> to <u>our parents</u>
   (4) remove the comma after <u>parents</u>
   (5) change <u>teachers</u> to <u>teacher's</u>

7. Sentence 3: **In the seventeenth and eighteenth centuries, a young man could not speak to a young woman until they had been properly introduced.**

   What correction should be made to this sentence?

   (1) remove the comma after <u>centuries</u>
   (2) change <u>speak</u> to <u>have spoken</u>
   (3) insert a comma after <u>woman</u>
   (4) change <u>had been</u> to <u>was</u>
   (5) no correction is necessary

8. Sentence 4: **Then the first move was hers since he could not speak to her until she had acknowledged his first.**

   What correction should be made to this sentence?

   (1) change <u>hers</u> to <u>her</u>
   (2) change <u>he</u> to <u>his</u>
   (3) change <u>her</u> to <u>them</u>
   (4) change <u>she</u> to <u>it</u>
   (5) change <u>his</u> to <u>him</u>

9. Sentence 5: **Today the rules are much less <u>rigid, but them do exist</u> in some fashion.**

   Which of the following is the best way to write the underlined portion of this sentence? If you think the original is the best way, choose option (1).

   (1) rigid, but them do exist
   (2) rigid but them do exist
   (3) rigid, but they do exist
   (4) rigid but they does exist
   (5) rigid, but them does exist

10. Sentence 6: **Recognizing and following it is important for acceptable social behavior.**

    What correction should be made to this sentence?

    (1) insert a comma after <u>following</u>
    (2) change <u>it</u> to <u>them</u>
    (3) insert a comma after <u>important</u>
    (4) change the spelling of <u>acceptable</u> to <u>exceptable</u>
    (5) no correction is necessary

Tip

Decide which person (first, second, or third) is appropriate for the meaning of a sentence; then use that person consistently throughout the sentence and paragraph.

Usage

Test-taking Strategy: Understanding Indefinite Pronouns

Indefinite pronouns do not refer to any specific person or thing. Some indefinite pronouns are singular, some are plural, and some can be either singular or plural. Indefinite pronouns are often difficult to match with verbs or other pronouns in the sentence so that they agree.

♦ The following indefinite pronouns are usually singular: *anybody, anyone, each, either, everybody, everyone, everything, neither, nobody, none, nothing, one, somebody, someone, something*

♦ The following pronouns are always plural: *both, few, many, several*

♦ The following pronouns may be either singular or plural, depending on their meaning in a sentence: *all, any, most, some*

Some test questions ask you to recognize whether indefinite pronouns are used correctly.

Try these sample items. Circle the best answer to each one. Then check your answers.

(1) In sports, everyone expect to win, and nobody expects to lose. (2) Few stops to think that in a game only one team can win.

1. Sentence 1: **In sports, everyone expect to win, and nobody expects to lose.**

   What correction should be made to this sentence?

   (1) replace expect with expects
   (2) replace expect with will expect
   (3) change the comma after win to a semicolon
   (4) change lose to loose
   (5) no correction is necessary

2. Sentence 2: **Few stops to think that in a game only one team can win.**

   What correction should be made to this sentence?

   (1) change stops to stop
   (2) insert a comma after think
   (3) change can to did
   (4) change win to have won
   (5) no correction is necessary

1. (1) Everyone is a singular indefinite pronoun which requires the singular verb expects.

2. (1) Few is an indefinite pronoun that is always plural; therefore, the plural verb stop is correct.

Directions: Circle the <u>best answer</u> to each item. <u>Items 1 to 5</u> refer to the following paragraph.

(1) Everybody who rides a bicycle needs to acknowlege that there is some danger and wear a helmet. (2) Experts say that helmets could prevent 85 percent of bike injuries and deaths. (3) No one should take the chance of being hurt or killed. (4) Some of the dangers cyclists face are reduced by helmets. (5) Most of the helmets manufactured today conform to approved safety standards; however, some of the styles available are not as well designed as they should be. (6) When your trying on a helmet, make sure it fits snugly and allows good peripheral vision. (7) Finally, when you fasten the chin strap, it should not come loose when we twist or pull it.

1. Sentence 1: **Everybody who rides a bicycle needs to acknowlege that there is some danger and wear a helmet.**

   What correction should be made to this sentence?

   (1) insert a comma after <u>Everybody</u>
   (2) change <u>needs</u> to <u>need</u>
   (3) change the spelling of <u>acknowlege</u> to <u>acknowledge</u>
   (4) insert a comma after <u>danger</u>
   (5) no correction is necessary

2. Sentence 4: **Some of the dangers cyclists face are reduced by helmets.**

   If you rewrote sentence 4 beginning with

   <u>Wearing helmets</u>

   the next word should be

   (1) faces
   (2) reduces
   (3) dangers
   (4) cyclists
   (5) some

3. Sentence 5: **Most of the helmets manufactured today <u>conform to approved safety standards; however, some of the styles available are</u> not as well designed as they should be.**

   Which of the following is the best way to write the underlined portion of this sentence? If you think the original is the best way, choose option (1).

   (1) conform to approved safety standards; however, some of the styles available are
   (2) conforms to approved safety standards; however, some of the styles available are
   (3) conform to approved safety standards; however, some of the styles available is
   (4) conform to approved safety standards, however, some of the styles available are
   (5) conform to approved safety standards, however; some of the styles available were

4. Sentence 6: **When your trying on a helmet, make sure it fits snugly and allows good peripheral vision.**

   What correction should be made to this sentence?

   (1) change <u>your</u> to <u>you're</u>
   (2) change <u>your</u> to <u>their</u>
   (3) insert a comma after <u>snugly</u>
   (4) change <u>allows</u> to <u>allow</u>
   (5) no correction is necessary

5. Sentence 7: **Finally, when you fasten the chin strap, it should not come loose when we twist or pull it.**

   What correction should be made to this sentence?

   (1) remove the comma after <u>Finally</u>
   (2) remove the comma after <u>strap</u>
   (3) replace <u>come</u> with <u>have come</u>
   (4) change <u>we</u> to <u>you</u>
   (5) change <u>it</u> to <u>them</u>

Items 6 to 10 refer to the following paragraph.

(1) When somebody feels sick all over and has a throat too sore to swallow water comfortably, she may have a strep throat. (2) This kind of sore throat is different from the sore throat everyone get with a common cold. (3) Strep throat is a serious infection, and they needs medical attention. (4) This infection can also lead to serious complications such as rheumatic fever if you do not treat it with antibiotics. (5) Many of it's victims are children who are exposed to this infectious disease in school or day care.

6. Sentence 1: **When somebody feels sick all over and has a throat too sore to swallow water comfortably, she may have a strep throat.**

   What correction should be made to this sentence?

   (1) change feels to feel
   (2) change feels to felt
   (3) change too to to
   (4) change she to they
   (5) no correction is necessary

7. Sentence 2: **This kind of sore throat is different from the sore throat everyone get with a common cold.**

   What correction should be made to this sentence?

   (1) change is to was
   (2) change the spelling of different to diferent
   (3) change get to gets
   (4) change get to got
   (5) insert a comma after get

8. Sentence 3: **Strep throat is a serious infection, and they needs medical attention.**

   Which of the following is the best way to write the underlined portion of this sentence? If you think the original is the best way, choose option (1).

   (1) is a serious infection, and they needs
   (2) is a serious infection; and they needs
   (3) is a serious infection, they needs
   (4) is a serious infection and it needs
   (5) is a serious infection, and it needs

9. Sentence 4: **This infection can also lead to serious complications such as rheumatic fever if you do not treat it with antibiotics.**

   Which of the following is the best way to write the underlined portion of this sentence? If you think the original is the best way, choose option (1).

   (1) if you do not treat it
   (2) if you did not treat it
   (3) if you have not treated it
   (4) if you do not treat them
   (5) if you, do not treat it

10. Sentence 5: **Many of it's victims are children who are exposed to this infectious disease in school or day care.**

    What correction should be made to this sentence?

    (1) change it's to its
    (2) change are to will be
    (3) insert a semicolon after children
    (4) change the spelling of disease to disese
    (5) insert a comma after school

Tip Don't be fooled by the indefinite pronouns, *everyone, everything*, and *everybody.* The words may look like they are plural, but they are singular.

Usage

Test-taking Strategy: Understanding Relative Pronouns

♦ A relative pronoun introduces a group of words that refers to a noun or another pronoun:

> The Statue of Liberty, <u>which</u> was a gift from France, greets all those who sail into New York harbor.

♦ The relative pronouns are:

> who and whom—referring to people and animals; <u>who</u> is a subject pronoun, and <u>whom</u> is an object pronoun
>
> which—referring to things, places, and animals
>
> that—referring to people, places, or things

Some test questions ask you to recognize whether relative pronouns are used correctly.

Try these sample items. Circle the <u>best answer</u> to each one. Then check your answers.

(1) People which watch television most of their spare time are called couch potatoes. (2) Those who we call couch potatoes would probably do well to turn off the television more often.

1. Sentence 1: **People which watch television most of their spare time are called couch potatoes.**

   What correction should be made to this sentence?

   (1) change <u>which</u> to <u>who</u>
   (2) insert a comma after <u>television</u>
   (3) change <u>are</u> to <u>is</u>
   (4) change the spelling of <u>potatoes</u> to <u>potatos</u>
   (5) no correction is necessary

2. Sentence 2: **Those who we call couch potatoes would probably do well to turn off the television more often.**

   What correction should be made to this sentence?

   (1) change <u>who</u> to <u>what</u>
   (2) change <u>who</u> to <u>which</u>
   (3) change <u>who</u> to <u>whom</u>
   (4) insert a comma after <u>potatoes</u>
   (5) no correction is necessary

---

1. **(1)** <u>Which</u> cannot refer to people. <u>Who</u> refers to people and is the subject pronoun that is needed in this sentence.

2. **(3)** <u>Whom</u>, an object pronoun, is needed in this sentence.

Directions: Circle the best answer to each item. Items 1 to 5 refer to the following paragraph.

(1) In the United States, the president, whom has the constitutional authority, can sign legislation into law or veto it. (2) A Congress that has enough votes can then override the veto to make the law take effect. (3) Some legislation which are very popular with everyone is passed by Congress and signed ceremoniously by the president. (4) The president sometimes signed a piece of legislation with many pens so that he can give them to people who supported the legislation. (5) Both Congress and the president often face the dillema of deciding which legislation to pass and sign.

1. Sentence 1: **In the United States, the president, whom has the constitutional authority, can sign legislation into law or veto it.**

   What correction should be made to this sentence?

   (1) change whom to which
   (2) change whom to who
   (3) change the comma after authority to a semicolon
   (4) insert a comma after legislation
   (5) no correction is necessary

2. Sentence 2: **A Congress that has enough votes can then override the veto to make the law take effect.**

   What correction should be made to this sentence?

   (1) change that to whom
   (2) change that to what
   (3) change has to had
   (4) insert a comma after votes
   (5) no correction is necessary

3. Sentence 3: **Some legislation which are very popular with everyone is passed by Congress and signed ceremoniously by the president.**

   What correction should be made to this sentence?

   (1) change which to who
   (2) change are to is
   (3) insert a comma after everyone
   (4) change passed to past
   (5) insert a comma after passed

4. Sentence 4: **The president sometimes signed a piece of legislation with many pens so that he can give them to people who supported the legislation.**

   What correction should be made to this sentence?

   (1) insert a comma after president
   (2) change signed to signs
   (3) change the spelling of piece to peace
   (4) replace pens with pen's
   (5) insert a comma after that

5. Sentence 5: **Both Congress and the president often face the dillema of deciding which legislation to pass and sign.**

   What correction should be made to this sentence?

   (1) insert a comma after Congress
   (2) change face to faces
   (3) change the spelling of dillema to dilemma
   (4) insert a semicolon after deciding
   (5) no correction is necessary

Tip

The pronouns *who* and *whom* are not always relative pronouns. When they are used to begin questions, they are called interrogative pronouns:
Who is knocking at the door?

Items 6 to 10 refer to the following paragraph.

(1) We are all concerned about our diets. (2) Chinese food, who uses less fat than other cuisines, is considered healthful. (3) Italian food uses a lot of olive oil, what is also considered a good diet choice. (4) Diets that rely on good vegetable oils, like peanut and olive oil, are better than diets that rely on animal fat. (5) Unlike many vegetable oils, animal fats causes our arteries to clog. (6) Actually, however, too much of any fat is not good for me.

6. Sentence 2: **Chinese food, who uses less fat than other cuisines, is considered healthful.**

   What correction should be made to this sentence?

   (1) change who to whom
   (2) change who to what
   (3) change who to which
   (4) remove the comma after cuisines
   (5) change is to are

7. Sentence 3: **Italian food uses a lot of olive oil, what is also considered a good diet choice.**

   What correction should be made to this sentence?

   (1) change uses to use
   (2) change what to which
   (3) change what to whom
   (4) change is to are
   (5) no correction is necessary

8. Sentence 4: **Diets that rely on good vegetable oils, like peanut and olive oil, are better than diets that rely on animal fat.**

   What correction should be made to this sentence?

   (1) change are to is
   (2) change that rely to what rely
   (3) change that rely to who rely
   (4) remove the comma after oil
   (5) no correction is necessary

9. Sentence 5: **Unlike many vegetable oils, animal fats causes our arteries to clog.**

   What correction should be made to this sentence?

   (1) change the spelling of vegetable to vegtable
   (2) change the comma after oils to a semicolon
   (3) change causes to caused
   (4) change causes to cause
   (5) replace our with your

10. Sentence 6: **Actually, however, too much of any fat is not good for me.**

    What correction should be made to this sentence?

    (1) remove the comma after Actually
    (2) remove the comma after however
    (3) replace too with to
    (4) insert a comma after fat
    (5) replace me with us

Tip

Choose correctly between *who* and *whom*. *Who* is a subject pronoun. For *who*, you could substitute another subject pronoun like *he, she, I, we,* or *they*. *Whom* is an object pronoun. You could substitute another object pronoun like *us, me, them, him,* or *her*.

♦ The word that a pronoun refers to is its antecedent:

> John bought new tires for his car.

Pronouns must agree in person (first person, second person, or third person) and number (singular or plural) with their antecedents.

> I wish to exercise my rights. (first person singular)
>
> People wish to exercise their rights. (third person plural)

♦ To avoid vague pronoun reference, make sure the antecedent of a pronoun clearly refers to a specific noun or pronoun:

> With prices going up, it makes a raise necessary. (Vague reference—it doesn't refer to a specific noun.)
>
> With prices going up, a raise is necessary. (correct)

♦ To make meaning clear, be sure a pronoun refers to only one antecedent:

> The supervisors told the workers that they couldn't meet. (Unclear reference—they can refer to supervisors or workers.)
>
> The supervisors told the workers that a meeting was not possible. (clear meaning)

Some test questions ask you to recognize whether relative pronouns are used correctly with their antecedents.

Try this sample item. Circle the best answer. Then check your answer.

(1) The assembly workers and the managers all think they know best how to run the company. (2) The company president gives their employees a voice in how the company is run.

1. Sentence 2: **The company president gives their employees a voice in how the company is run.**

What correction should be made to this sentence?

(1) change president to President
(2) change gives to give
(3) change their to her
(4) change their to its
(5) change is to was

---

1. **(3)** The plural pronoun their does not agree with its antecedent, president, in number. The singular pronoun her is needed.

Directions: Circle the best answer to each item. Items 1 to 5 refer to the following paragraph.

(1) Writing routine business letters is not easy, which is why many people avoid the task. (2) However, if you learn some basic principles, they say you can write good letters. (3) Everyone can improve their business letters. (4) A writer can tell readers what they want to say by using these principles. (5) Put the main idea of the letter in a short first paragraph. (6) Put all details in middle paragraphs and close with a short paragraph. (7) Write clearly and definitely about the ideas that you want to comunicate.

1. Sentence 1: **Writing routine business letters is not easy, which is why many people avoid the task.**

   Which of the following is the best way to write the underlined portion of this sentence? If you think the original is the best way, choose option (1).

   (1) easy, which is why
   (2) easy, that is why
   (3) easy; which is why
   (4) easy, therefore,
   (5) easy which is why

2. Sentence 2: **However, if you learn some basic principles, they say you can write good letters.**

   What correction should be made to this sentence?

   (1) insert a comma after some
   (2) change the spelling of principles to principals
   (3) change the comma after principles to a semicolon
   (4) change they to experts
   (5) no correction is necessary

3. Sentence 3: **Everyone can improve their business letters.**

   What correction should be made to this sentence?

   (1) change can to can have
   (2) change improve to improved
   (3) insert a comma after improve
   (4) change their to its
   (5) change their to his or her

4. Sentence 4: **A writer can tell readers what they want to say by using these principles.**

   Which of the following is the best way to write the underlined portion of this sentence? If you think the original is the best way, choose option (1).

   (1) A writer can tell readers what they want
   (2) A writer can tell readers what they want,
   (3) A writer can tell readers what he or she wants
   (4) A writer should tell readers what they want
   (5) A writer will tell readers what they want

5. Sentence 7: **Write clearly and definitely about the ideas that you want to comunicate.**

   What correction should be made to this sentence?

   (1) change the spelling of definitely to defenately
   (2) insert a comma after ideas
   (3) change that to what
   (4) change want to wants
   (5) change the spelling of comunicate to communicate

Items 6 to 10 refer to the following paragraph.

(1) Bridge is a popular card game. (2) Each of the four players in a bridge game is paired; they play with a partner. (3) The partners sit across from each other, and when the cards are dealt, they bid for the right to determine which suit will be trumps. (4) They also agree to win a certain number of tricks. (5) The named suit, who might be hearts, spades, diamonds, or clubs, becomes the trump. (6) Or the highest bidders can also say they wants to play with no suit as trump. (7) Then each player had played one card at a time; the highest card wins each time. (8) The winning side either takes all the cards they said they would, or stops the other side from taking their cards.

6. Sentence 2: **Each of the four players in a bridge game is paired; they play with a partner.**

   What correction needs to be made to this sentence?

   (1) insert a comma after players
   (2) change the semicolon to a comma
   (3) change they play to each one plays
   (4) change they to them
   (5) change they to their

7. Sentence 3: **The partners sit across from each other, and when the cards are dealt, they bid for the right to determine which suit will be trumps.**

   Which of the following is the best way to write the underlined portion of this sentence? If you think the original is the best way, choose option (1).

   (1) dealt, they bid
   (2) dealt; they bid
   (3) dealt, and they bid
   (4) dealt they bid,
   (5) dealt, they had bid

8. Sentence 5: **The named suit, who might be hearts, spades, diamonds, or clubs, becomes the trump.**

   Which of the following is the best way to write the underlined portion of this sentence? If you think the original is the best way, choose option (1).

   (1) suit, who might
   (2) suit, what might
   (3) suit, whom might
   (4) suit, which might
   (5) suit; who might

9. Sentence 6: **Or the highest bidders can also say they wants to play with no suit as trump.**

   What correction should be made to this sentence?

   (1) change bidders to bidder
   (2) change they to he or she
   (3) change they to them
   (4) change wants to want
   (5) insert a comma after suit

10. Sentence 7: **Then each player had played one card at a time; the highest card wins each time.**

    What correction should be made to this sentence?

    (1) change had played to has played
    (2) change had played to plays
    (3) change had played to play
    (4) change time to times
    (5) change the semicolon to a comma

Sentence Structure

Test-taking Strategy: Understanding Fragments and
Run-On Sentences

♦ Fragments are incomplete sentences that are missing a subject, a verb, or
both. Consequently, they don't express a complete thought:

> Before the war. (fragment)
> Before the war, life was pleasant. (complete sentence)

♦ Another type of fragment is a dependent clause punctuated as a sentence.
It has a subject and verb, but it begins with a subordinate conjunction.
Attaching the dependent clause to the related independent clause will
correct the fragment:

> Although the night was beautiful. (fragment)
> Although the night was beautiful, it was cold. (Complete sentence)

♦ A run-on sentence has two or more independent clauses put together
without linking words or proper punctuation:

> The night was beautiful it was cold. (run-on)

A run-on sentence can be corrected in the following ways: (1) using a
period to create separate sentences, (2) using a semicolon, (3) using a
comma and a coordinating conjunction, or (4) using a semicolon, a
conjunctive adverb, and a comma:

> (1) The night was beautiful. It was cold.
> (2) The night was beautiful; it was cold.
> (3) The night was beautiful, but it was cold.
> (4) The night was beautiful; however, it was cold.

Some test questions ask you to recognize ways to correct sentence
fragments and run-on sentences.

Try this sample item. Circle the best answer. Then check your answer.

(1) Celebrities often have difficulty living
private lives. (2) So many photographers and
fans. (3) They invade their lives. (4) The
celebrities need the publicity, but they hate the
invasion of their privacy.

(1) fans. They invade
(2) fans. They invaded
(3) fans, they invade
(4) fans; invade
(5) fans invade

1. Sentences 2 and 3: **So many
   photographers and fans. They invade
   their lives.**

   Which of the following is the best way to
   write the underlined portion of these
   sentences? If you think the original is the
   best way, choose option (1).

1. **(5)** Sentence (2) is a fragment because it
   lacks a verb. Combining the two sentences
   provides the verb <u>invade</u> to correct the
   fragment.

Directions: Circle the best answer to each item.
Items 1 to 4 refer to the following paragraph.

(1) More and more Americans are telecommuting. (2) Telecommuting working from home instead of at a company's offices. (3) Telecommuting saves travel time and even saves money on work clothes telecommuters simply walk into their office spaces at home, wearing whatever is comfortable, and begin working at their own desks. (4) Companies telecommuting for various reasons, such as increased worker morale and less need for office space. (5) Because telecommuters need to be sure, however, that they consider all aspects of working at home.

1. Sentence 2: **Telecommuting working from home instead of at a company's offices.**

   Which of the following is the best way to write the underlined portion of this sentence? If you think the original is the best way, choose option (1).

   (1) Telecommuting working
   (2) Telecommuting, working
   (3) Telecommuting is working
   (4) Telecommuting and working
   (5) Telecommuting since working

2. Sentence 3: **Telecommuting saves travel time and even saves money on work clothes telecommuters simply walk into their office spaces at home, wearing whatever is comfortable, and begin working at their own desks.**

   Which of the following is the best way to write the underlined portion of this sentence? If you think the original is the best way, choose option (1).

   (1) clothes telecommuters simply walk
   (2) clothes, telecommuters simply walk
   (3) clothes telecommuters, simply walk
   (4) clothes; telecommuters simply walk
   (5) clothes telecommuters simply walk,

3. Sentence 4: **Companies telecommuting for various reasons, such as increased worker morale and less need for office space.**

   Which of the following is the best way to write the underlined portion of this sentence? If you think the original is the best way, choose option (1).

   (1) Companies telecommuting
   (2) Although companies telecommuting
   (3) Companies always telecommuting
   (4) Some companies telecommuting
   (5) Companies allow telecommuting

4. Sentence 5: **Because telecommuters need to be sure, however, that they consider all aspects of working at home.**

   What correction should be made to this sentence?

   (1) change Because telecommuters to Telecommuters
   (2) change Because to Since
   (3) change the comma after sure to a semicolon
   (4) add a comma after aspects
   (5) no correction is necessary

Items 5 to 9 refer to the following paragraph.

(1) Technology exists that allow us to determine where anything is located on Earth. (2) Global positioning. (3) Although global positioning lets you use a hand-held receiver to determine exactly where you are. (4) Hikers and drivers would never get lost, and any stolen car could be found easily. (5) Objects, whether they are moving or stationary could be located. (6) The equipment would use precise data beamed to Earth by the satellites.

5. Sentence 1: **Technology exists that allow us to determine where anything is located on Earth.**

   What correction should be made to this sentence?

   (1) remove exists
   (2) insert a comma after exists
   (3) change allow to allows
   (4) change the spelling of determine to determin
   (5) insert a semicolon after is

6. Sentence 2: **Global positioning.**

   Which of the following is the best way to write the underlined portion of this sentence? If you think the original is the best way, choose option (1).

   (1) Global positioning.
   (2) It is called global positioning.
   (3) Called global positioning.
   (4) It is called, global positioning.
   (5) Its called global positioning.

7. Sentence 3: **Although global positioning lets you use a hand-held receiver to determine exactly where you are.**

   What correction should be made to this sentence?

   (1) change Although global to Global
   (2) add a comma after receiver
   (3) change where to which
   (4) insert at after are
   (5) no correction is necessary

8. Sentence 4: **Hikers and drivers would never get lost, and any stolen car could be found easily.**

   What correction should be made to this sentence?

   (1) change the comma to a semicolon
   (2) insert a comma after and
   (3) change could to can
   (4) change found to find
   (5) no correction is necessary

9. Sentence 5: **Objects, whether they are moving or stationary could be located.**

   What correction should be made to this sentence?

   (1) change the spelling of whether to weather
   (2) change are to will be
   (3) insert a comma after moving
   (4) change the spelling of stationary to stationery
   (5) insert a comma after stationary

Tip If a sentence fragment begins with a subordinate conjunction, you can often correct the fragment by eliminating that subordinate conjunction and capitalizing the next word.

Sentence Structure

Test-taking Strategy: Understanding Misplaced Modifiers

Misplaced modifiers confuse readers because they seem to refer to the wrong word or to more than one word in a sentence.

♦ Place a word or phrase as close as possible to the word it modifies in a sentence:

The car ran off the road and hit the tree <u>as it was trying to get back on the road.</u> (misplaced modifier)

The car ran off the road and, <u>as it was trying to get back on the road</u>, it hit the tree. (correctly placed modifier)

Some test questions ask you to recognize the best way to correct misplaced modifiers.

Try these sample items. Circle the <u>best answer</u> to each one. Then check your answers.

(1) A wart appeared on my hand that I wanted removed. (2) The doctor decided to remove it easily.

1. Sentence 1: **A wart <u>appeared on my hand that I wanted removed.</u>**

   Which of the following is the best way to write the underlined portion of this sentence? If you think the original is the best way, choose option (1).

   (1) appeared on my hand that I wanted removed.
   (2) appeared that I wanted removed on my hand.
   (3) that I wanted removed appeared on my hand.
   (4) that I wanted appeared removed on my hand.
   (5) on my hand appeared that I wanted removed.

2. Sentence 2: **The doctor <u>decided to remove it easily.</u>**

   Which of the following is the best way to write the underlined portion of this sentence? If you think the original is the best way, choose option (1).

   (1) decided to remove it easily.
   (2) will decide to remove it easily.
   (3) will decide to remove it, easily.
   (4) easily decided to remove it.
   (5) decided, easily to remove it.

   ---

   1. **(3)** The clause <u>that I wanted removed</u> must be moved so that it modifies <u>wart</u>, not <u>hand</u>.

   2. **(4)** The word <u>easily</u> must be moved so that it tells how the doctor decided.

Directions: Circle the best answer to each item. Items 1 to 5 refer to the following paragraph.

(1) When traveling long distances, you must be prepared with children. (2) They need many items to keep him happy in cars. (3) Games, books, pillows, and snacks. (4) However, people in cars that are overflowing with children often dont seem to have much fun. (5) Sometimes you see by the side of the road a car with a family that has broken down. (6) Traveling with children is hard, but having car trouble makes it a nightmare.

1. Sentence 1: **When traveling long distances, you must be prepared with children.**

   Which of the following is the best way to write the underlined portion of this sentence? If you think the original is the best way, choose option (1).

   (1) distances, you must be prepared with children.
   (2) distances you must be prepared with children.
   (3) distances with children, you must be prepared.
   (4) distances you must with children be prepared.
   (5) distances; you must with children be prepared.

2. Sentence 2: **They need many items to keep him happy in cars.**

   What correction should be made to this sentence?

   (1) change need to needs
   (2) change items to item's
   (3) change him to them
   (4) insert a comma after happy
   (5) no correction is necessary

3. Sentence 3: **Games, books, pillows, and snacks.**

   What correction should be made to this sentence?

   (1) remove the comma after Games
   (2) insert a comma after and
   (3) add many after and
   (4) insert are useful after snacks
   (5) no correction is necessary

4. Sentence 4: **However, people in cars that are overflowing with children often dont seem to have much fun.**

   What correction should be made to this sentence?

   (1) change the comma to a semicolon
   (2) change that to what
   (3) change are to were
   (4) change are to had been
   (5) change dont to don't

5. Sentence 5: **Sometimes you see by the side of the road a car with a family that has broken down.**

   Which of the following is the best way to write the underlined portion of this sentence? If you think the original is the best way, choose option (1).

   (1) by the side of the road a car with a family that has broken down.
   (2) by the side of the road a car that has broken down with a family.
   (3) a car with a family that has broken down by the side of the road.
   (4) a family by the side of the road with a car that has broken down.
   (5) a family with a car by the side of the road that has broken down.

Lesson 11

Items 6 to 10 refer to the following paragraph.

(1) The art of quiltmaking has enjoyed a new popularity, which was once nearly forgotten. (2) Today, people make quilts for artistic plesure. (3) In the past, quilts were made for different reasons. (4) The first quilts, for example were made for warmth. (5) The first quilter used scraps of cloth to make a quilt which was scarce. (6) Later, specially manufactured fabrics, were used by quilters to create a variety of designs.

6. Sentence 1: **The art of quiltmaking has enjoyed a new popularity, which was once nearly forgotten.**

   If you rewrote sentence beginning with

   The art of quiltmaking, which

   the next words should be

   (1) nearly once
   (2) was once
   (3) enjoyed
   (4) was enjoyed
   (5) has popularity

7. Sentence 2: **Today, people make quilts for artistic plesure.**

   What correction should be made to this sentence?

   (1) remove the comma after Today
   (2) insert who after people
   (3) change make to made
   (4) insert a comma after quilts
   (5) change the spelling of plesure to pleasure

8. Sentence 4: **The first quilts, for example were made for warmth.**

   What correction should be made to this sentence?

   (1) insert a comma after example
   (2) change were to was
   (3) insert a comma after made
   (4) change the spelling of warmth to wormth
   (5) no correction is necessary

9. Sentence 5: **The first quilter used scraps of cloth to make a quilt which was scarce.**

   Which of the following is the best way to write the underlined portion of this sentence? If you think the original is the best way, choose option (1).

   (1) cloth to make a quilt which was scarce.
   (2) cloth; to make a quilt which was scarce.
   (3) cloth, which was scarce, to make a quilt.
   (4) quilt to make a cloth which was scarce.
   (5) cloth which was scarce; to make a quilt.

10. Sentence 6: **Later, specially manufactured fabrics, were used by quilters to create a variety of designs.**

    What correction should be made to this sentence?

    (1) remove the comma after Later
    (2) remove the comma after fabrics
    (3) change were to was
    (4) insert a comma after quilters
    (5) change the spelling of variety to vareity

Tip Ask yourself who or what a modifying word or phrase describes. Then make sure the modifier is placed in the sentence as close as possible to whatever it describes.

Sentence Structure

LESSON 12

Test-taking Strategy: Understanding Dangling Modifiers

♦ Dangling modifiers confuse readers because the sentence is missing an appropriate subject for the modifying phrase:

<u>Looking down at the valley</u>, the colors were beautiful. (dangling modifier)

<u>Looking down at the valley</u>, <u>we saw</u> that the colors were beautiful. (corrected sentence)

Who was looking down? In the original sentence, the phrase modifies <u>colors</u>. However, it doesn't make sense that colors were looking down at the valley.

♦ To fix a dangling modifier, provide a subject for it or create a subordinate clause:

<u>Walking to the office</u>, the police car pulled over the red car. (dangling modifier)

<u>Walking to the office</u>, <u>I saw</u> the police car pull over the red car. (corrected by providing a subject)

<u>While I was walking to the office</u>, I saw the police car pull over the red car. (A subordinate clause corrects the dangling modifier.)

Some test questions ask you to recognize the best way to correct dangling midifiers.

Try these sample items. Circle the <u>best answer</u> to each one. Then check your answers.

(1) Hoping for a vacation, our work was taking longer. (2) Daydreaming, our office tasks piled up.

1. Sentence 1: **Hoping for a vacation, our work was taking longer.**

   What correction should be made to this sentence?

   (1) change the spelling of <u>Hoping</u> to <u>Hopping</u>
   (2) change <u>Hoping for a vacation</u> to <u>Because we were hoping for a vacation</u>
   (3) remove the comma
   (4) change the comma to a semicolon
   (5) no correction is necessary

2. Sentence 2: **Daydreaming, our office tasks piled up.**

   If you rewrote sentence 2 beginning with

   <u>Our office tasks piled up</u>

   the next words should be

   (1) as daydreaming
   (2) daydreaming
   (3) and daydreamed
   (4) as we daydreamed
   (5) so they daydreamed

   ---

   1. **(2)** The subordinate clause contains the subject needed to fix the dangling modifier.

   2. **(4)** The dangling modifier is provided with the subject <u>we</u>.

Focus on Skills • Usage and Sentence Structure